Contents

All about spiders

There are billions of spiders on Earth. They live in houses and gardens, ponds and caves, rainforests, deserts and the Arctic. They survive in almost every possible **habitat**, except for **Antarctica** and the oceans.

So far, scientists have found about 38,000 different **species** of spiders. New species are being discovered all the time so there may be many more than this. Every spider catches animals for food. The largest eat snakes, lizards and birds. The smallest eat tiny flies.

Many spiders live among plants in parks and gardens.

Raft spiders live near marshes and ponds.
They catch insects on the water's surface.

This book is all about spiders. It tells you how they spin silk, how they produce their young, and all the different ways they catch and kill their **prey**.

Leg span

0 cm   25 cm

Biggest and smallest

The world's largest spider is the Goliath tarantula, shown here. It has a **leg span** of more than 25 cm. The smallest is the Samoan moss spider. With a leg span of under 0.5 mm, it can hardly be seen.

Spiders and their relatives

Spiders belong to a large group of animals called **arachnids**. All arachnids have four pairs of legs and a body divided into two parts. Other members of the group include harvestmen, scorpions, mites and ticks. They are close relatives of spiders.

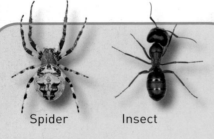

Spider   Insect

Not an insect!

What's the difference between a spider and an insect? Spiders have two parts to their body and eight legs. Insects have three parts to their body and six legs. Most insects have **antennae** and wings; spiders never do.

Harvestmen have very long, thin legs and look like spiders. However, their bodies are built in a different way, and they do not spin silk.

Scorpions have long, **segmented** bodies, a large pair of claws and a curved tail tipped with a sting.

Mites are tiny, with short legs and round bodies. Many of them live on animals and irritate their skin.

Ticks cling on to animals and feed on their blood. They can spread disease.

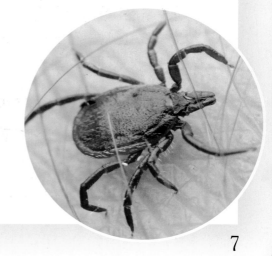

A spider's body

A spider's body is made
up of two main segments:
the head and the **abdomen**.
The two parts are joined
by a slender waist.

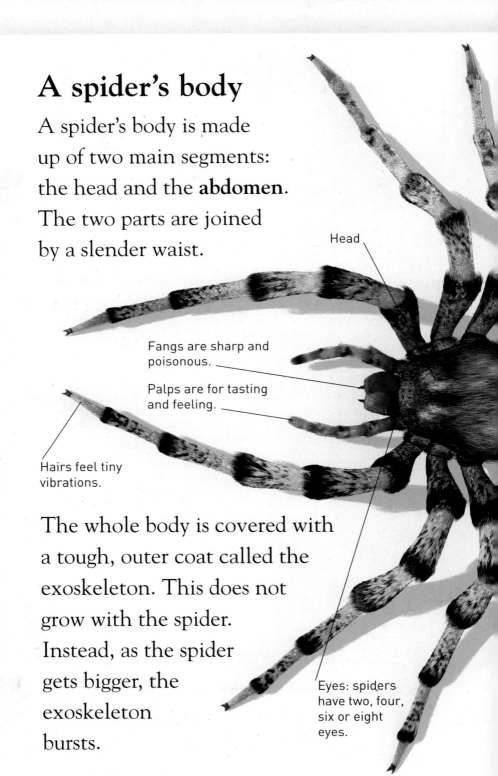

Head

Fangs are sharp and
poisonous.

Palps are for tasting
and feeling.

Hairs feel tiny
vibrations.

Eyes: spiders
have two, four,
six or eight
eyes.

The whole body is covered with
a tough, outer coat called the
exoskeleton. This does not
grow with the spider.
Instead, as the spider
gets bigger, the
exoskeleton
bursts.

Old coat

Underneath there is a new, larger coat. The spider crawls out of the old coat and leaves it behind. This is called moulting.

Legs are long and segmented.

Abdomen

Feet at the end of each leg give spiders a good grip.

Spinnerets produce silk.

Speedy spiders

Spiders are very quick thanks to their eight long legs. The giant house spider holds the record for the fastest spider. It can move at 53 centimetres per second!

Spider silk

Spider silk is an amazing material. It is finer than hair, stronger than steel and stretchy like elastic. It is waterproof, light enough to float and can even be **recycled**.

Spiders use silk in all sorts of ways: to build their webs, line their **burrows**, protect their eggs and wrap up their prey. They also make silk safety lines to escape from danger or jump distances.

A jumping spider leaps into the air from its silk safety line.

Thick and thin

A spider's silk is not always the same. It can be thick or thin, wet or dry, sticky or woolly. It all depends on how it will be used.

A garden spider pulls the silk from its spinnerets
to wrap a fly it has caught in its web.

A spider makes silk inside its body in special
organs called glands. The runny silk squirts out
of holes in the **spinnerets**, like water out of a
showerhead. The spider then uses one of its legs
to pull and twist the different strands into a
single, solid thread.

Spider webs

Many spiders make sticky webs to catch
flies and other insects. Spiders spin webs in
a variety of shapes, such as flat sheets, long
tubes and round **orb webs**.

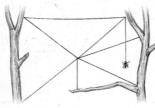

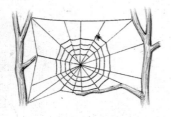

Making an orb web

1. The spider connects two
twigs with strong thread and
pulls it down.

2. It adds spokes and fixes
them firmly.

3. Then it spins a sticky spiral
to hold the spokes in place.

An orb web takes about an hour to make.
The lacy threads are soon spoilt by dust,
wind or rain, so most spiders spin a new web
every day. The old one does not go to waste;
the spider eats it and recycles the silk.

Record breaker

The golden orb-weaver spider spins the largest orb web in the world. It builds webs up to a metre wide and strong enough to catch frogs and birds, as well as all kinds of insects.

A helpless fly is rolled up in silk by a garden spider.

Deadly fangs

When an insect flies into a web, the spider feels it straight away through the fine hairs on its legs. It darts out quickly to bite its prey.

Nearly all spiders produce **venom**. As they bite their prey, venom pumps out through their hollow fangs and enters the victim's body. The venom does two things: it stops the creature moving and begins to **digest** its body, turning it into a kind of soup. The spider then sucks it up.

If a large insect flies into the web, the spider wraps it quickly in silk before biting it. This prevents the insect from breaking free. If the spider isn't hungry, it will keep its prisoner waiting, and return to eat it later.

A black and yellow garden spider wraps up a grasshopper before it can get away.

Types of fangs

Some spiders have fangs that point towards each other, like pincers. They are good for seizing prey. Other spiders have fangs that point downwards, like daggers. These spiders have to lift their head up and strike down to attack.

Hunting spiders

Not all spiders spin webs; some hunt for a meal. Hunting spiders are strong and fast, and have sharp eyesight to spot their prey.

Jumping spiders are deadly hunters. They have brilliant eyesight and can jump up to 50 times their body length to catch their prey.

A jumping spider prepares to pounce on its insect prey.

Amazing eyes

Jumping spiders have two big eyes on the front of their head and smaller eyes around the sides. The smaller eyes spot prey and judge how far away it is. The large eyes give a clearer picture.

A fishing spider feels for prey in the water.

The fishing spider hunts at the river's edge. Its front legs rest on the surface of the water, feeling for the movement of tadpoles, frogs and fish in the water.

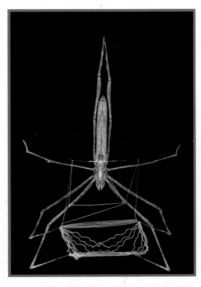

A net-casting spider prepares to catch its prey.

Net-casting spiders hunt at night. They hold a small flat web between their legs and throw it over insects like a net as they pass by.

Ambush!

Some spiders are sneaky hunters and **ambush** their prey. They hide somewhere safe and keep very still. Then, when they see their prey, they jump out and grab it!

The trapdoor spider digs a burrow with a trapdoor on the top. At night, it opens the door a crack and waits for an insect to pass by. Then it jumps on the insect and drags it back into its burrow.

A trapdoor spider leaps out of its burrow to grab an unlucky insect.

If you look closely, you can see the fang of a purse-web spider that has just stabbed this cranefly from beneath.

The purse-web spider makes a long silk tube, and covers it with bits of soil. The spider hides inside the tube and waits for its prey to walk over it. Then it stabs its prey through the soft, silk walls before dragging it inside.

Camouflage

Many spiders use **camouflage** to fool their prey. The crab spider hides inside flowers to catch insects that come to feed. They do not see the spider because it can change colour to match the petals on the flower.

Dangerous spiders

Nearly every species of spider has its own kind of venom, but only about 100 species are dangerous to humans. Venom affects humans in different ways. Some venom affects the muscles and causes painful **cramps**. Other venom causes damage around the bite itself, leaving scars that take months to heal. Luckily, most bites can be treated with special medicines called anti-venoms.

Black widow spider

Watch out for: red markings on its abdomen

Found in: warm parts of the world including southern USA

Leg span: 3.8 cm

Effect of venom: breathing problems, muscle cramps and sickness.

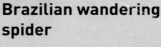

Brazilian wandering spider

Watch out for: large, brown hairy body

Found in: tropical rainforests of South America

Leg span: 12 cm

Effect of venom: severe pain. Can be fatal.

Sydney funnel-web spider

Watch out for: large, shiny, brown-black body

Found in: eastern Australia

Leg span: 6 cm

Effect of venom: sickness and sweating. Can kill in under two hours.

Brown recluse spider

Watch out for: violin-like markings on its head

Found in: Southern USA and Mexico

Leg span: 1–2 cm

Effect of venom: leaves a deep wound that is slow to heal.

Finding a mate

Most spiders live alone. When it is time to mate, a male finds a female by following a scent she leaves on her silk.

The male spider is often much smaller than the female. If he is not careful, she could mistake him for prey and eat him. So as he approaches the female, he may give her an insect to eat or tap a friendly signal on her web. If she accepts him, the two spiders mate.

Eggs for life

After mating just once, the female black widow spider can lay eggs for the rest of her life.

A week or two later, the female lays her eggs. She wraps them in a thick **cocoon** and then puts them somewhere safe to hatch. Most females leave or die before they see their young.

Little and large: a male golden orb-weaver spider carefully approaches a female much larger than himself.

Tiny wasp
spiderlings
hatch out
together.

Baby spiders

Baby spiders are called **spiderlings**. They hatch out
of their eggs together but soon spread out to look
for food. If they didn't, they would eat each other!
Each tiny spiderling makes a line of very fine silk,
called gossamer, and uses it to float away on the
breeze. This is called ballooning.

Most spider mothers do not care for their young,
but the wolf spider mother is different. She carries
her egg cocoon around with her. After hatching,
the spiderlings climb on her back.

Wolf spiderlings cling to their mother as she runs and hunts.

They ride there for a week or so until they are big enough to hunt. If one of them falls off, the mother stops whatever she is doing and helps it back.

Ballooning

Ballooning helps spiders to reach new places. Most only travel a few metres, while others travel long distances. Some get caught up on aeroplanes; others float across the sea to remote islands.

Spider defences

Spiders are food for birds, lizards, centipedes, wasps and many other animals. Most spiders escape from their enemies by dropping away on a line of silk. Others have special **defences**.

Some spiders copy ants by walking on six legs, and holding up the other two so that they look like antennae. Birds don't like the taste of ants, so they leave these spiders alone.

A jumping spider copies an ant.

A tarantula defends itself by flicking hairs on the face of an enemy. The hairs have sharp little hooks, which stick into the eyes and nose of the enemy and make them feel itchy and sore.

Ant

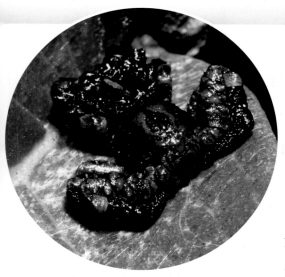

The bird-dropping spider looks like… a bird dropping! This is great camouflage and most animals give it a miss.

A bird-dropping spider looks nothing like a spider!

Deadly enemy

Spiders' defences don't always work. The spider-hunting wasp is a spider's deadly enemy. It will sting a spider so it cannot move, and then lay its eggs inside its body. The eggs hatch out into hungry **grubs**, which eat the spider alive.

A spider-hunting wasp (on the left) drags a wolf spider back to its burrow.

Spiders help us

Many people do not like spiders, but they help us in many ways. They eat billions of the mosquitoes, cockroaches and other insects that cause disease. They also eat many pests in gardens and on farms; without them swarms of insects would feed on our crops and people would starve.

Grasshoppers are a pest on farms because they eat crops. Spiders are a natural form of pest control.

Tasty tarantulas

In some parts of South America and south-east Asia, people eat roasted tarantulas. They have a nutty flavour.

Scientists in Germany work to copy spider
silk and produce it in the laboratory.

Spiders may be very
useful in the future.
Scientists are studying
spider venom in the hope
of using it in **insecticides**,
and replacing harmful
chemicals. They are also

Healing webs

Stories from thousands
of years ago tell how
people once used
spiders' webs to help
heal their wounds.

studying how spiders make silk. This amazing
material may have many uses. We may use it
for car seat belts, parachutes and bullet-proof
clothing. One day, doctors may even sew up
wounds using spider silk!

Glossary

abdomen The back part of an arachnid's body.

ambush To lie in wait and attack an animal by surprise.

Antarctica The ice-covered land around the South Pole.

antennae The pair of feelers on an insect's head.

arachnids A group of animals that have four pairs of legs and a body divided into two parts.

burrows Holes or tunnels dug by an animal for shelter.

camouflage The colour or markings of an animal that help it blend in with its surroundings.

cocoon The silky covering a spider spins to protect its eggs.

cramps Sudden, strong pains in the muscles.

defences The ways that animals protect themselves from attack.

digest To break down food so that it can be used by the body.

grubs The tiny creatures that hatch out of insects' eggs. Also called larvae.

habitat The place where an animal usually lives.

insecticides The sprays and powders that farmers use to kill insect pests.

leg span The distance between two legs on the opposite sides of a spider.

orb webs Webs with a round, circular shape.

organs The parts of an animal's body, such as the eyes or brain, that do a particular job.

prey Animals that are hunted and killed by other animals for food.

recycled Used again or made new from used materials.

segmented Made up of different parts or segments.

species A group of living things that share similar features and can breed together.

spiderlings Baby spiders.

spinnerets The parts of a spider's body that produce silk.

venom The poison that a spider injects when it bites.

Index